THE SEASONS

Sue Crawford

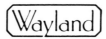

Topics

All the words that appear in **bold** are explained in the glossary on page 30.

Cover A frosty winter's morning in Oxfordshire, England.

Editors: Clare Chandler and Joan Walters

First published in 1987 by

First published in 1987 by
Wayland (Publishers) Limited
61 Western Road, Hove
East Sussex BN3 1JD, England

© Copyright 1987 Wayland (Publishers) Ltd

British Library Cataloguing in Publication Data

Crawford, Sue
    The seasons. – (Topics).
    1. Seasons – Juvenile literature
    I. Title   II. Series
    574.5'43   QH48

    ISBN 1–85210–093–1

Phototypeset by
Kalligraphics Ltd, Redhill, Surrey
Printed and bound in Belgium
by Casterman S.A., Tournai

Contents

What are Seasons?

Have you ever wondered why many parts of the world have four seasons, and why Spring, Summer, Autumn and Winter follow in the same pattern each year? Or why it is Summer in Australia when it is Winter in Britain?

The Ancient Greeks and Romans believed that we have Summer and Winter because of an argument between the gods. Ceres, the goddess of the harvest, was angry

The women in this painting, called 'The Seasons' by Walter Crane, are dressed to show Spring, Summer, Autumn and Winter.

A painting by Pietro Bianchi of Ceres, the goddess of the harvest. The ancient Greeks and Romans believed that she was responsible for Summer and Winter.

with Pluto, the god of the underworld, for stealing her daughter Persephone. Pluto agreed to let Persephone return from the underworld for six months each year. During these months Ceres is happy and sends sunshine and crops to the land. For the other half of the year Ceres cries, the weather is cold and dismal and nothing will grow.

A medieval picture showing fruit being harvested at the end of Summer.

Our **ancestors** began to connect **astronomy** with the seasons when they saw that the stars seemed to change their positions in the night sky as the year went by. By drawing up charts of star patterns, people were able to make calendars which divided the year into months and seasons. Calendars helped farmers decide when to plant and harvest their crops.

Lunar calendars depend on the movement of the Moon as it spins round the Earth. Every time there is a new Moon it is the start of a lunar month and after 28 days the lunar month ends with a full Moon.

Nowadays most countries use the solar (Sun) calendar which is worked out by counting how long it takes for the Earth to **orbit** the Sun: 365 and a quarter days, or one year. This is divided up into 12 months of unequal length.

The reason we have different seasons is that the Earth tilts as it orbits the Sun. While the bottom half of Earth (the Southern **hemisphere**) tilts towards the Sun

This map shows how the Earth is divided by climate and seasons.

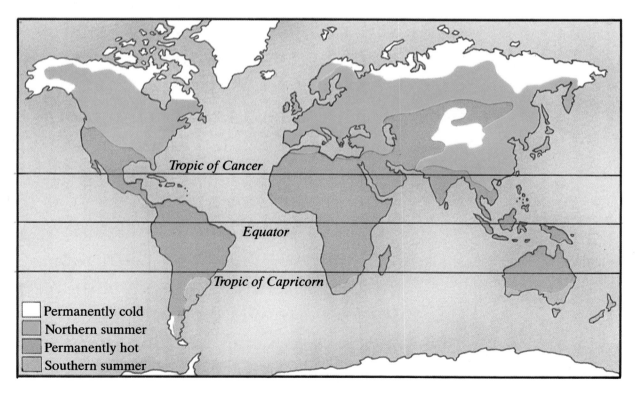

Tropic of Cancer

Equator

Tropic of Capricorn

Permanently cold
Northern summer
Permanently hot
Southern summer

and has Summer, the top half (the Northern hemisphere) tilts away from the Sun and has Winter. For the second half of the year the Northern hemisphere has its chance to be closer to the Sun and it is Winter on the other side of the world, in the Southern hemisphere.

Map makers draw an imaginary line around the middle of the Earth which divides the Northern from the Southern hemisphere. It is called the Equator. They also draw two imaginary lines to the north and south of the Equator called the Tropics of Capricorn and Cancer. The region between the Equator and the Tropics of Capricorn and Cancer is known as the **Tropics**. The Tropics do not have four seasons, their climate is always hot. Some tropical countries have a wet season when the **Monsoon** winds blow in from the sea, and a dry season when the winds blow from across the hot land.

These men in Bangladesh are wearing straw covers to protect themselves from the Monsoon rain while they work in the rice fields.

At the top and bottom of the Earth, the North and South Poles, it is always cold and icy. People living near the North Pole have nearly 24 hours of daylight in the Summer and no night time, whereas in the middle of Winter they have 24 hours of night. Meanwhile at the South Pole the months of daylight and darkness are exactly opposite. Imagine living in the **Arctic**, sometimes called the Land of the Midnight Sun, and spending part of the year in continual sunlight!

In the Arctic, and in Antarctica, you can still see the sun at midnight during the summer.

Changing Seasons

This diagram shows how the tilt of the Earth, as it orbits the sun, affects the amount of light and heat that reach the Earth at different times of the year, so giving us the changing seasons.

Many people live in the middle **latitudes**, where there are four seasons of about three months each: Spring, Summer, Autumn and Winter. As the seasons change the days grow either shorter or longer. Around 21 June countries in the Northern hemisphere are at

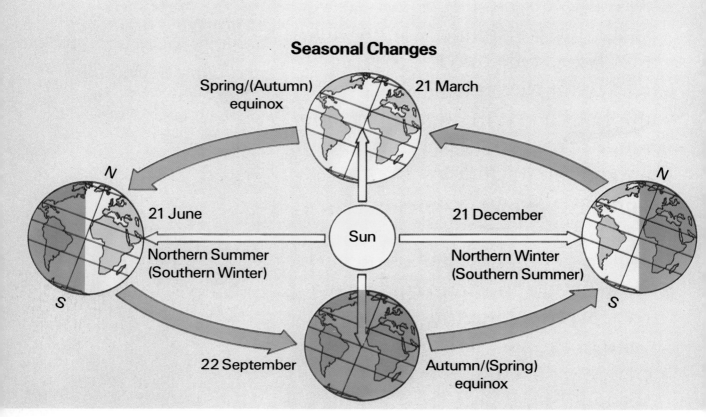

Seasonal Changes

Spring/(Autumn) equinox — 21 March

N

21 June

Northern Summer (Southern Winter)

Sun

21 December

Northern Winter (Southern Summer)

N

S

S

22 September

Autumn/(Spring) equinox

their most extreme tilt towards the Sun so they have the shortest night and the longest day (about 19 hours of daylight) in their calendar. After this day, which marks the beginning of Summer and is called the Summer **solstice** or Midsummer, the days grow shorter until the shortest day or Winter solstice. This is known as the first day of Winter and falls around 21 December.

In the middle latitudes, there are two days in the year, called equinoxes, when the hours of daylight and darkness are exactly equal. Spring begins with an equinox around 21 March and the Autumn equinox is usually on 22 September. In the Southern hemisphere the equinoxes, like the solstices, are the opposite way round. For example if you left Australia in the Spring and flew to Canada, you would find it was Autumn when you arrived!

*These two pictures of the same area of countryside show the difference between Winter (**above**) and Spring (**below**).*

Seasons in various countries can be quite different from each other because everyday patterns of weather also depend on the local **landscape.** Countries between the Equator and the Tropics of Capricorn and Cancer tend to have hot Summers, whereas countries near the Poles, especially if they are inland or mountainous, have cold Winters with snow and ice.

Winter in Alaska is long and harsh. The Inuit people travel across the snow by snowmobile and sledge.

In the Spring plants start to grow strongly again and buds and blossom appear on the trees. Gradually the countryside turns from brown to green as the days grow warmer, longer and lighter. Many animals give birth to their young and farmers plant the crops they will harvest at the end of the Summer.

During the summer corn and

Many animals give birth to their young in Spring. These baby rabbits are two weeks old.

In the Summer, when it is warm and sunny, many people go to the seaside for a holiday. This is Yalta in the USSR.

other crops ripen, flowers are at their most colourful and many types of fruit and vegetable are ready to pick. In the Summer months people often wear lighter clothes, spend more time outdoors and take holidays in the countryside or by the sea.

Falling leaves are the most obvious sign that Autumn has arrived, and in the USA this season is known as the Fall. Trees lose water through their leaves so by shedding them in Autumn they are able to slow down their growth to survive throughout the Winter when the ground is frozen and their roots cannot draw up **sap**.

In some parts of the world Autumn is a very colourful season. This is Autumn in Vermont, USA.

Winter is a tough season for animals. Food is scarce and the weather can be very harsh. This female blackbird is feeding on windfall apples.

In the Winter much of the countryside is bare and brown. Nothing much grows, snow may fall and the ground often freezes, making it hard for birds and other animals to find food. When the weather becomes cold, windy and wet, people spend more time indoors. Towards the end of Winter, Spring gradually arrives. As the first bulbs and shoots push out of the hard ground, the **cycle** of the seasons begins once again.

Seasonal Movements

As the seasons change, many kinds of animals make long and difficult journeys from one part of the world to another. They go either to escape from the cold, or to return to a place especially good for breeding, or to find fresh supplies of food. These regular movements are called migration.

Because of the severe climate in the Arctic, reindeer move south in the Autumn to find food. In the Spring, when the ice begins to melt, they return to the fresh grass of the northern forests.

Large antelopes called gnus, who live in the African grasslands, form into herds at the start of the dry season in March and move north-west in search of new grazing land. Lions, hunting dogs and jackals follow the herd to catch and eat old or sick animals who fall behind.

In Norway, reindeer herds migrate to escape the cold northern winter.

As soon as the rainy season begins in South America and Africa, millions of frogs and toads make long and difficult journeys from dry places to the swamps because they must lay their eggs in water. No one is sure how frogs find their way back to the same pools each year, but they may be guided by their strong sense of smell.

About half of the 8000 different kinds of bird in the world migrate.

This sign warns motorists that toads are crossing the road to return to their breeding pools in Spring.

Each Spring they travel enormous distances to build their nests and hatch their young, often in exactly the same spot as the previous year. At the end of Summer they make a return journey to spend the Winter in a place where the **climate** is warmer and food is easier to find. For centuries people have wondered how they know when to leave and how they find their way.

Scientists have suggested that the extra daylight of the long Summer days releases a chemical in a bird's

Tree swallows in New Jersey, USA, gather together in Autumn before they make the long journey south where it is warmer and food is more plentiful.

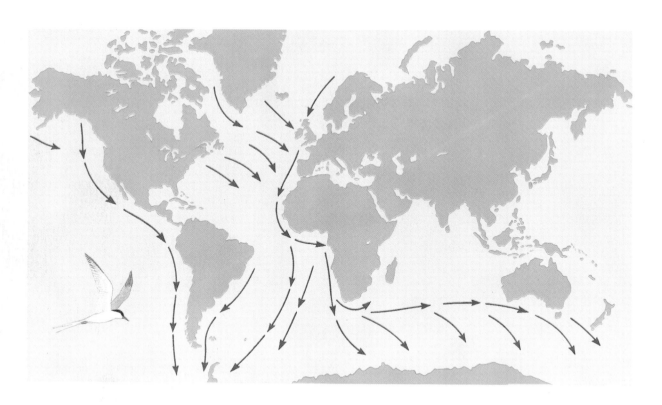

This map shows the routes taken by the Arctic tern when it migrates to Antarctica for the southern summer.

brain which makes it feel restless and ready to make a journey. It also causes the bird to store extra fat in its body as fuel for the long flight it will make in the Autumn. The Arctic tern flies the furthest of all birds. In Autumn it leaves the Arctic to spend the northern Winter on the **Antarctic** coastline. In Spring it returns to the Arctic to nest. The round trip is an amazing 35000 kilometres.

Seasonal migrations also go on underwater. When Summer turns to Autumn, or Winter turns to Spring, winds and sea currents become stronger and help fish travel long distances to find new food supplies or suitable breeding grounds.

Instead of migrating, some smaller mammals, such as hares and shrews, survive the Winter by hibernating. This means eating plenty during the Summer and Autumn to build up reserves of fat, then digging a burrow and spending the coldest weather in a deep sleep underground.

Above *Garden dormice hibernate through the winter.*

Salmon leap up fast-flowing rivers to return to the place where they were born and where they too will breed.

21

Celebrating the Seasons

Druids celebrate the Summer solstice at an ancient monument called Stonehenge in England.

Each season has it own special festivals and celebrations. Some of these are very ancient. A ring of giant-sized stones called Stonehenge, in England, was probably built by our ancestors as a place for worshipping the Sun at the Summer solstice on 21 June.

On 1 May, called May Day, it is an English tradition for people to dance around a maypole.

The return of Spring after Winter is a special cause for celebration. 1 May has traditionally been a time for country people to celebrate the growth of the new **vegetation** by building a Maypole decorated with flowers and leaves and dancing around it. Nowadays people often keep up **pagan traditions** like this for fun.

These children are painting eggs to give as Easter gifts.

Some festivals seem to belong to a particular season but are really linked to religious events. The word Easter comes from the name of an ancient goddess whose feast day was held at the Spring equinox. However Easter is now the time Christians celebrate the resurrection (rebirth after death) of Jesus Christ. Spring is a time of new beginnings and one Easter custom is for people to give each other gifts of painted or chocolate eggs, as a sign of new life.

Jewish people hold a festival called the Passover in the Spring. This looks back to the time when Jews were slaves in Egypt and God freed them and sent Moses to lead them to a new land. A Hindu Spring festival called Holi falls on the day between March and April when there is a full moon. Huge bonfires are lit and grain and coconut are cooked to celebrate the Earth's fertility. Everyone has fun dressing up and acting out traditional stories about the Hindu god Krishna.

Holi is a Hindu festival celebrated in Spring. As part of the festivities people throw coloured water and red powder at each other.

Just before the rainy season in July, some countries near the Equator have flower and rain festivals to give thanks for the beauty of the Earth and to encourage the rain to come. The **Buddhist** festival of Pansa takes place in parts of India and China during the three months of the rainy season.

These people are taking part in a water festival in Burma.

During Autumn, many religions hold festivals to give thanks for a successful harvest. Christian churches may be decorated with flowers, fruit and loaves of bread shaped like sheaves of corn. The Chinese hold a Moon festival in September to celebrate the brightest full moon of the year. At nightfall they greet the moon with a colourful procession of lanterns in

Christian churches are decorated with fruit and vegetables during the Harvest festival which is celebrated in Autumn.

27

These Chinese children in London are celebrating the brightest full moon in September by holding a moon festival.

all shapes and sizes made by the children.

The main Winter festival, which many countries hold on 25 December, is Christmas. Christmas is a Christian festival recalling the birth of Jesus, son of God, almost 2000 years ago. On Christmas Eve

Christian churches hold services at midnight and people sing carols.

Although Jesus was born in a hot country, Christmas is now closely associated with the season of Winter. In Norway seven kinds of 'thaw' biscuit are baked to eat over the festival season. Norwegian tradition claims that the heat of all the ovens baking biscuits helps the Winter snow to thaw!

A little girl and her mother prepare special biscuits to celebrate Christmas.

Glossary

Ancestors People we are descended from who lived long ago.

Antarctic The most southern region of the world.

Arctic The most northern region of the world.

Astronomy Study of the stars and planets.

Buddhist Buddhists are followers of a man they called Buddha who lived 2500 years ago.

Climate Weather in a particular place, which is affected by how close it is to the Equator or the North or South Poles. It also depends on whether the place is near sea or mountains and what grows there.

Cycle Series of events following each other round in a circular pattern which recurs again and again.

Hemisphere Half of the Earth. The Northern and Southern hemispheres are divided from each other by an imaginary line called the Equator.

Landscape What a particular piece of land looks like. This depends on where it is, what rocks lie under the ground and what the land is being used for.

Latitudes Lines drawn around maps of the Earth, parallel with the Equator, which measure how far a place is either North or South of the Equator.

Lunar To do with the moon.

Monsoon Seasonal wind blowing across the Indian Ocean from the south west and bringing rain in Summer.

Orbit The curved path followed by a planet or satellite around the earth or sun.

Pagan traditions Customs from the period before Christianity when many gods and spirits were worshipped.

Sap Watery juice in plants. In Spring sap rises in tree trunks and helps new leaves to grow.

Solstice The two days in the year when the Sun is furthest from the Equator.

Tropics Hot, damp regions lying between the Tropics of Capricorn and Cancer.

Vegetation Everything that grows out of the ground, such as edible and inedible plants, trees and bushes.

Books to Read

Faiths and Festivals by Martin
    Palmer (Ward Lock
    Educational, 1984).
The Seasons by Robin Kerrod
    (Franklin Watts, 1975).
Animal Migration by Federico
    Columbo (Burke Books, 1981).
Festivals (audio-visual pack)
    (Mary Glasgow Publications,
    1982).
Spring by David Lambert
    (Wayland, 1986).
Summer by Ralph Whitlock
    (Wayland, 1986).
Autumn by Ralph Whitlock
    (Wayland, 1987).

Winter by Ralph Whitlock
    (Wayland, 1987).
Animal Migration by Malcolm
    Penny (Wayland, 1987).

Books for Older Readers

Countryside by Heather Angel
    (Rainbird, 1983).
Man in Society by James Mitchell
    (Windward, 1980).
World Mythology by Rex Warner
    (Octopus, 1979).

Picture Acknowledgements

The illustrations in this book were supplied by: Bridgeman Art Library 4, 5; Bruce
Coleman 9, 12, 15, 16, 17, 18, 21, 22; Hayward Art Group 7, 27; Hutchison Library 8,
25, 26, 28; Wendy Meadway 20; Oxford Scientific Films: cover, 11 (D. Thompson), 13
(G.I. Bernard), 19 (P. Murray, Animals Animals); Malcolm Walker 10; Zefa 14, 23,
24, 29.

Index